ALLON
A short history

CW00402107

by

Peter Ostle

with maps and sketches by David Lush

British Library Cataloguing in Publication Data

A catalogue record for this book is available from the British Library

ISBN 978-0-9572412-7-5

Published in 2014 by:- P3 Publications,13 Beaver Road, Carlisle, Cumbria, CA2 7PS.

Printed in Wales by:- Gomer Press, Llandysul Enterprise Park, Ceredigion SA44 4JL.

Front Cover: The Reading Rooms with their original open colonnade.

The Romans and the saltpans

Swarthy Hill, or Bluebell Hill as it is known locally, lies just about two miles south of Allonby. On top of the hill, there are the remains of a Roman fort; at its foot, lie the saltpans.

Hadrian's Wall runs from Wallsend, on the east coast, to Bowness-on-Solway. The Emperor also ordered the building of a line of forts along the coast, stretching from Bowness south to St. Bees Head. The 'Milefort' at Saltpans is the best preserved of the smaller fortifications.

The Senhouse Museum, in Maryport, tells the full story of the Roman occupation of the area and contains many fine relics from that period. It is near the site of a major fort known to the Romans as Aluna.

Salt making was an important industry, all along the Solway coast, from medieval times. The remains on the shore here are considered to be the best preserved direct-boiling salt works in England. They were constructed in 1634 and continued in operation until the late 1700s.

There are two large, circular stone-lined pits. Seawater would be pumped firstly in to smaller tank and then to the larger, higher one. From here the water would flow into the 'pan houses'. There it would be gently heated by coal fires in shallow iron vessels until it evaporated, leaving the salt crystals behind.

At low tide, traces of the system for collecting the seawater can still be seen. At the other side of the road are the foundations of several buildings which were originally the salt workers' homes and stables. The salt would be delivered to wholesalers, known as Badgers, by horse and cart. The coal would arrive the same way, probably from early drift mines around Bulgill and Oughterside.

An aerial view by Simon Ledingham.

For many years the saltpans were a caravan and camping site.

Until 1823, salt was heavily taxed in England. Salt Officers collected the duty from both manufacturers and importers. One of these officers, John Smith, is buried in Crosscanonby churchyard.

His tombstone shows him sitting at his desk, adding up the tax due.

The inscription tells us he was Salt Officer for the Netherhall and Crosscanonby pans for twenty-nine years.

He died, aged 64, in 1730.

Early days

It seems probable that 'Allonby' was, originally, the name of a farm rather than a village.

John Denton wrote the first known history of Cumberland around 1610. He devotes only a few lines to Allonby, saying:

"Adam, son of Odard de Wigton, gave to Alane of Hensingham, his third son, a piece of ground by the sea where he first erected his capital messuage [Principal residence] and named it Allanby now that township so called to this day. . ." This probably happened around 1160, when Henry II established Norman rule in Carlisle.

Thomas Denton's *'Perambulation of Cumberland'* was prepared in 1687. It devotes a little more space to "Allanbie . . . the first village in this [Bromfield] parish, being a little fishers-town standing upon the seashore, opposite to Scruffell in Galoway." He says William Blennerhasset has "here a small demesne of £30 a year." A demesne is land occupied by the owner, rather than let to a tenant. He had another farm at Mealo which was worth £40 a year, a corn mill, fishing rights and some salt pans rented out for £20 a year. The Beeby family had two farms at Bowscale and Crookhurst. There were also a few 'customary tenants' – these were probably farmhands, fishermen or workers at the salt pans.

So, a picture emerges of a tiny, scattered community around four large farms, with the one at Allonby being the local manor house. The entries in the Bromfield Parish records confirm this. In the ten years from 1654, thirteen children from Allonby were baptised there. This compares to more than forty from Westnewton, the neighbouring hamlet, a few miles inland.

A hundred years later, the picture had changed completely; there seems to have been a population explosion. Allonby now had its own church. Between 1774 and 1783, one-hundred-and-seventy-four children were baptised there. Around twenty more births are recorded in the Quakers' registers during this ten year period.

Allonby was by then a proper, self-contained village and had grown in importance as a port. In 1745, Bonnie Prince Charlie took over Carlisle and declared his father King of England at the cross there. During these upheavals, the local Quarter Sessions were held at Allonby in Jane Sim's house – probably a pub.

At the Easter sessions in 1746, Thomas Robson petitioned the crown for payment of his expenses. He had hired horses, men and a carriage to carry some artillery, used by the Duke of Cumberland when he re-took Carlisle castle from the rebels. Robson had brought them to Allonby for shipment south, the journey taking two days and two nights. It must have been fairly heavy stuff!

Allonby was also becoming a holiday resort. In November 1787, the *Cumberland Pacquet* carried an advert offering the lease of the 'London Apprentice' inn for sale. Included in the deal was a bathing machine.

Allonby in the 18ᵗʰ century. The original church or 'Chapel of Ease' can be seen on the extreme right of the engraving.

Allonby Mill (above) is now an antiques shop. The position of the weir and millpond which serviced it can be seen on the 1860 O.S. map. The water wheel was probably located in the small lean-to building beside the weir. The buildings to the left of the mill have been demolished; they may have been the miller's home.

In former times, the beck was much broader and shallower than it is today as can be seen in the picture opposite. The present deep channel was dug by POWs during the Second World War.

The present mill building dates from the nineteenth century. It must stand on the site of an earlier mill which, like most of Allonby's early homes and farms would have been a 'Clay Dabbin'. These were constructed from a timber frame filled with a mixture of clay, straw, gravel and, sometimes, crushed sea shells set on a foundation of cobbles from the shore.

In Garden Lane, the garage at Rainford House was originally a clay dabbin cottage. At some time it was extended upwards by adding a stone-built gable. You can see the join where the

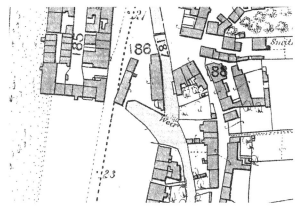

present owner has restored the clay structure with antique bricks. A piece of the original clay and gravel has been 'framed' on the side wall of the garage.

A typical Clay Dabbin, accommodating both a family and their livestock.

The Quakers

George Fox founded The Society of Friends, the Quakers, around 1650. He visited Carlisle in 1653, Abbeytown in 1657 and gained many followers throughout north Cumberland.

In Allonby, Robert Sibson and Francis Hayton were among the first to be 'convinced of ye truth'. About 1656, they joined a number of other converts who lived further up the coast, around Mawbray. In these early days, the Quakers met in each other's houses or the open air. Over the next few years, they were joined by several other families from Allonby. These included the Stubbs, the Martindales, the Elwoods, and the Beebys; they were mostly fairly prosperous farmers.

The Quakers refused to take any oath, believing that one standard of truthfulness should apply at all times. They also refused to pay their 'Tithes', a tax on agricultural land levied to support the local church and vicar.

These principles landed the early Quakers in a great deal of hot water with the local magistrates. Many were imprisoned at Carlisle and others were heavily fined. In 1660, one Allonby man, Francis Hayton was imprisoned for thirty-two weeks, after refusing to pay his tithes. Two years later, he was fined 3/4d. for refusing to swear in the manor court.

However, most of the Allonby Quakers seem to have escaped the worst of this persecution. They must have settled down pretty well by May 1665 when they conducted an open air wedding somewhere on Mawbray Banks. Thomas Elwood from Allonby married Mary Ritson from Mawbray. The Marriage Certificate is preserved at Friends' House in London. It is one of the very earliest Quaker wedding records to have survived anywhere in the country.

By 1689, the group were large enough and confident enough to build their first proper Meeting House somewhere near Beckfoot. Then, in 1701, the Allonby Friends decided they needed a place of their own. They bought a cottage at the north end of the village which they extended in 1732 to accommodate 120. This Meeting House was used continuously every Sunday for over two-hundred-and-fifty years.

The Quakers also built a walled burial ground near North Lodge.

By the 1980s, the Meeting House was beginning to show its age. The windows were jammed shut, the floor was rotten and it was very damp. The members obtained a grant from the Rowntree Foundation and, altogether, raised about £3,000 for repairs. Work began but more and more structural problems were discovered. Finally, the funds ran out and there seemed to be no alternative but to close the building.

The Meeting officially closed in July 1991. The building was sold five years later and converted into a private house.

The Meeting House in the 1970s. There were no windows on the seaward side of the building. Sketch by David Butler from his book 'Meeting Houses of the Lake Counties'

Fishing

There have been fishermen in Allonby since the 1680s. The fleet of boats grew rapidly from then on and seems to have reached its peak size in the late 1700s and early 1800s. The main catch was always herring. Two methods of preserving the fish for transport to the market were used – salting and kippering.

The Beeby family established their fish yards sometime in the mid-1700s. Here, the herring would be gutted, salted and then packed into barrels. The barrels were made in a cooperage on the premises by Richard Harker, Daniel Beeby's brother-in-law and business partner.

The Beeby family had their own fishing boat the 'Lion'. In 1785 they exchanged it for a larger vessel the 'Hope'. This sloop was built in Allonby and registered 35 tons. In 1789, they invested in the 'Assistance' of 63 tons. This boat was built for them in Maryport. Her name was an allusion to the fact that Nicholas hoped she would assist in supporting his growing family.

The Beeby's fish yards can be seen in the background of this postcard view. On the foreshore, the hull of the 'Esther' one of Allonby's last fishing wherries awaits the ship-breakers.

Not all the herring caught were salted. Another Allonby family, the Costins, turned the rest into kippers!

Their operation was located on the other side of the green in the area known as 'The Hill' which, in more recent times, was home to the Riding School.

In the three-storey smokehouse, a wood-burning open hearth was located on the first floor. The herring could be hung in this room or, on the floor above, in the roof space. The chimney passed through both floors and flagstones could be removed from it to allow the smoke to belch out into either of the rooms as required.

When the kippers were ready, the louver shutters on the front of the building would be opened to allow the smoke to escape.

Herring were not the only catch. Right up to the war years, cod, skate, lobsters and prawns as well as shrimps were landed at Allonby. The skate were known locally as Bluets. They were big fish but not quite as tasty as the thornback skate. They were caught on a line, laid out to sea from east to west, baited with herring or plaice, and fixed in the sand by an anchor. Any hard pull on the line moved the anchor so that the flukes dug into the sand. Using this method a fisherman could tell, from the position of the anchor, if there was a fish on the line.

An old water colour of the Kipper Factory.

11

The Baths

In July 1834, the *Carlisle Journal* reported "a great deal of company at Allonby, enjoying the healthful breezes of that pleasant place. As in former years, there are still complaints of the want of indoor amusements for whiling away the tedium of a wet day. There is neither public library, public news-room, billiard table nor any other place of resort to form a common lounge for visitors . . . in our variable climate some provision should be made."

Later that year, a few local people with 'a number of gentlemen from further afield' got together and raised £1,800 in £5 shares to buy some land and erect a bath house. The committee accepted plans submitted by Thomas Nelson, Carlisle's leading builder. There would be a basement floor with warm, cold, sulphur and vapour baths and, above this, a 'noble apartment' 50 feet long and 25 feet wide. Tenders were invited from local builders.

In May 1835, the local press reported 'workmen are now rapidly proceeding with the erection'. By July 1836, the baths were open.

The baths were fitted out in marble and were supplied with water drawn from the sea in pipes by a small steam engine. The engine's furnace also heated the water for the hot baths. All this state-of-the-art technology was up and running several years before the Maryport and Carlisle Railway opened!

The large 'Promenade Room' looked over the sea with an iron balustrade which ran the whole length of the building. There was also a smaller reading room. The *Journal* concluded 'the terms of admission are very moderate to all parts of the building and must prove a very great accommodation to visitors'.

In 1856, Allonby Baths faced new competition; a new seaside resort was taking shape, just a few miles away. Silloth had, not only, a fine selection of modern hotels and boarding houses but also an attractive set of sea water baths.

It seems that the Allonby baths never recovered their popularity after this. In August 1862, a rather sad notice appeared in the local papers. A meeting of shareholders was called 'for the purpose of taking into consideration an offer which has been made for the purchase of the land and buildings' and to consider liquidating the debts and winding up. It was signed by Thomas Williamson, the secretary.

The offer seems to have come from Joseph Pease, MP who had also financed the Reading Rooms. The baths building was converted into a boarding house and, by the turn of the century, became a private residence which it has remained ever since. It is a Grade II listed building.

In 1836, the *Carlisle Journal* listed some of those who had already visited the baths. It was an assembly which would not have disgraced Downton Abbey and included:-

---

Sir Wilfrid Lawson, Bart. of Brayton Hall and Lady Lawson (née Polking-ton-Senhouse)

Sir Francis Fletcher Vane, Bart., Lady Vane and family with the Lady Dowager and Miss Sophia Vane of Armathwaite Hall.

C.S. Featherstonhaugh (pronounced Fanshaw), Esq. and family, Kirkoswald.

Field Marshal Sir Hew Dalrymple Ross, G.C.B., Royal Artillery and Lady Elizabeth Margaret Ross who may have also been visiting her family, the Grahams, at the Stone House, Brampton.

Mrs. G Ferguson and family of Hougton Hall and Joseph Ferguson, Esq., cotton manufacturer, of Carlisle.

G.C. Mounsey, Esq., Mayor of Carlisle and family.

The Rev. H. Lowther and family, Disington.

Not all the visitors had local roots, also there were: Lieutenant Robinson, R.N. and family, London; Captain Steel and family, Calcutta; Mrs and Miss Crawford, Crawford Castle, Scotland; The Rev. Mr Wilkinson of Halifax and Mr Bedford of London.

ALLONBY BATHS

THE PROPRIETOR begs to return his sincere thanks for the very liberal patronage bestowed upon him since he entered upon the above Institution, and hopes by strict attention to the comfort and convenience of his patrons, to merit a continuance of the same.

Hot, Cold, Shower and Plunge Baths,

Can be had at any moment from Six a.m., to Ten p.m.

HOT BATHS	COLD BATHS
One ... 1s. 6d.	One ... 1s. 0d.
Six ... 7s. 6d.	Six ... 5s. 0d.

Slipper and Shower together 9d.

The Ladies' Baths are under the charge of experienced, female attendants.

Furnished Apartments above the Bath Rooms, all with delightful Sea Views.

R. SHADWICK, Proprietor

N.B. – Only pure Sea Water is kept on these premises.

Sir Hew Dalrymple Ross

Sir Francis Fletcher Vane

Temperance

By the mid-1800s, Allonby had seven pubs, two wine and spirit merchants and its own brewery and maltings. It provided an easy target for the early members of the Temperance Movement. The 'evils of drink' among the working classes became a middle-class obsession in the second half of the century. The Movement's leaders came from the clergy and lay preachers of the non-conformist chapels. The establishment of a new Congregational church in Allonby probably gave it a big boost.

The Congregational Chapel

Jabez Tunnicliff, a Baptist minister from Leeds, formed the Band of Hope in 1847. The Allonby branch must have been formed in its very early days. The Band was an organisation for young people who were required to 'sign the pledge' and promise to abstain from all intoxicating liquors. It provided some wonderful social activities for Allonby's kids over many, many years. There were football, cricket and tennis teams. In the winter, there were meetings with talks, sing-songs and occasional magic lantern shows. However, the highlight of the year for all the young members was 'The Trip'.

In July 1886, John Walker, a local Quaker, noted in his diary: "Band of Hope Picnic, Heathfield. 149 persons, 13 carts". Forty years later, the trips were still going strong. The late Eric Laws remembered one, in the 1920s, to Brayton Hall, near Aspatria, for a picnic and cricket match.

The Temperance Movement gathered considerable support around Allonby. Its greatest triumph came in 1862 with the opening of the new Reading Rooms. This was to be 'a rival to the ale house' and provide for 'the real education of the working man'.

Local people were invited to subscribe for shares but the £200 raised fell far short of the capital required. Joseph Pease stepped in to save the day. Eventually he contributed over £1,000 to the project and commissioned Alfred Waterhouse, a 32-year-old Quaker architect from Manchester, to design the building. The building contract was awarded to Thomas Osborne of Cowgate and the joinery work was carried out by Thomas Longcake of Silloth.

Originally, the Reading Rooms stood over an open Italian style piazza where people could shelter from inclement weather. Above this colonnade were the actual reading room and a library. A house was attached for the headmaster of the nearby British School. Later, the open colonnade was bricked-in and converted into a billiard and games room.

The Reading Rooms served the people of Allonby for more than one hundred years. They became home to a collection of natural history specimens. During the Second World War, they were used by the WVS for the preparation of camouflage netting for the armed forces. During the Festival of Britain, in 1951, they hosted a 'Festival of Antiques'.

By the 1970s, usage had declined and maintenance was a problem. The trustees decided to sell the building and use the proceeds to modernise the village hall. It was purchased by Philip Harker, a local businessman, who proposed turning it into a Motor Cycle Museum. His plans were turned down by the local authority and the Reading Rooms then stood, unoccupied for thirty years. The fabric began to deteriorate and, after a severe storm, part of the roof came away, bringing the gable end with it.

At last, in 2005, the local council agreed to partial demolition and conversion to residential use. The work began quickly but was hampered by delays and spiralling costs. Finally, in 2013, the new owners moved in and could enjoy one of the most beautifully situated homes in England!

JOSEPH PEASE
(1799 – 1872)

Pease took over the Stockton and Darlington Railway from his father in the 1820s. He was the largest colliery owner in the South Durham coalfield. In 1832, he became Britain's first Quaker MP and was a prominent member of the anti-slavery movement. His wife, Emma, was a member of the Gurney banking family of Norwich and a cousin of Elizabeth Fry, the prison reformer.

ALFRED WATERHOUSE
(1830 – 1905)

Waterhouse became one of the Victorian era's most prominent architects. Among the buildings he designed were Manchester Town Hall, The Natural History Museum in London, Liverpool Royal Infirmary and Strangeways Prison. His brother, Edwin, was an accountant. His firm is still in business – Price Waterhouse.

North Lodge

North Lodge about 1910. The building on the right was the coach house and the wall on the left surrounds the Quaker burial ground.

Joseph Pease's cousin, Thomas Richardson, built North Lodge in the 1830s; he had married an Allonby girl, Martha Beeby, in 1799.

Thomas Richardson was a Quaker and one of the original partners in Richardson, Overend and Gurney, a prominent banking house in the City of London. He also held shares in both the Stockton & Darlington Railway and Stephenson's Locomotive Works. He was one of the original proprietors of Middlesbrough Docks and was a great benefactor of the Friends' Schools at both Brookfield, near Wigton and Ayton in North Yorkshire

The central pavilion of the lodge was to provide a holiday home for the Richardsons. At either side of this, were six cottages for local widows and spinsters who were to live there rent free and receive £5 per year from an endowment fund which Thomas provided. The building is still in use as low-cost housing.

Thomas Richardson

18

Christ Church

Allonby was originally part of Bromfield Parish. Until the mid-eighteenth century local people had to travel almost six miles inland to attend a service or get married. Then, in 1743, the Rev. William Thomlinson built a 'Chapel of Ease' for them. Thomlinson's family were Lords of the Manor at Bromfield although the reverend gentleman's own parish was in County Durham.

The chapel was a simple structure with thirty-four pews. In 1845 it was demolished and a new building was constructed on the same site. It formed the nave of the present church. The chancel, sanctuary and choir stalls were added in 1885. Some further changes to the interior were made shortly after the Second World War.

The schoolroom was re-built in 1837 and served as a day school until the early twentieth century. After this it was used as a Sunday School. Allonby became a parish in its own right in 1906.

Services are held at the church at 9.00am on most Sundays throughout the year. At other times, the building is usually locked but admission can be arranged by one of the church wardens. Contact details and current service times are displayed in the Sunday School window.

The 1900s

A visitor to Allonby, at the dawn of the twentieth century, would see the village very much as we know it today.

There were two main differences. The beck was crossed by a cast iron bridge, built in 1848 as part of the Maryport to Wigton turnpike road and the shore was an industrial site.

At the south end of the village, the Twentyman family operated a ship-breaking business. John Twentyman, a retired mariner, started this in the 1880s but business peaked in the early 1900s as steel replaced wood in the construction of new vessels. Several local men and boys were employed there. The wood was salvaged for use by local builders.

There was great excitement in the village in 1903 when the barque 'Hougoumont' ran aground there. No lives were lost but the ship's cargo was scattered all over the shore. The villagers mounted a 'salvage operation'. The crates contained tins of salmon, peaches and pears but were unlabelled. The only way to tell which was which was by shaking them; if the contents moved, it was fruit. A good time, and a few good meals, were had by all!

In November 1905, the beck was swollen after heavy rain. A traction engine, hauling a steam-driven fairground ride, approached the old cast iron bridge from Maryport. It never made it to the other side. The bridge cracked under the weight and the vehicles ended up in the beck! A new stone bridge was built and is still in use today.

Apart from these episodes of excitement, life went on and everybody enjoyed their visit to Allonby!

Sport was always an important part of Allonby life. As well as an annual sports day, there were regular tennis and cricket matches on the green. In 1912, a 9-hole golf course was created at the north end of the village.

The Sunshine Home

Lord Howard of Penrith declared the Sunshine Home open on 17th August 1933. Its building was financed by Ann Robinson-Harrison of Scalesceugh Hall, near Carlisle. It was originally named in memory of her husband, John, a director of Gow Harrison, the Clydeside ship builders.

For almost sixty years, it provided a fortnight's holiday for under privileged children from all over the county.

The John Robinson-Harrison Memorial
Fresh-Air Fortnight Home,
ALLONBY-ON-SOLWAY, CUMBERLAND.

NON-SECTARIAN.   NON-POLITICAL.
Open February to November inclusive each year.

OFFICERS.
President—
Mrs. ROBINSON-HARRISON.

Vice-Presidents—
The Lady MABEL HOWARD.   Lady LITHGOW.
Mrs. HERBERT ATKINSON.

Management Committee—
Mrs. ROBINSON-HARRISON.   Miss JOSEPHINE CHANCE.
The Lady MABEL HOWARD.   Miss DONALD.
Lady LITHGOW.   Mrs. INGLIS.
Mrs. H. ATKINSON.   Mrs. IREDALE.
Mrs. R. C. CHANCE.   Miss MOUNSEY-HEYSHAM.
Mrs. F. STEPHENSON.

The home's original prospectus.

The home was open each year from Easter until October and provided accommodation for between eight and ten children. Originally, boys and girls were separated for alternate fortnights but, from the early 1970s, they mixed together. The children would arrive on a Monday and stay for eleven days, leaving on a Friday. This gave the staff a week-end off every other week.

Great emphasis was placed on the health of the children. A local doctor always acted as the home's Honorary Medical Officer. The first of these was Dr J.W. Crerar of Maryport. In later years, Dr John Leiper of Carlisle took over and, eventually, became chairman of the management committee.

The home always relied on voluntary contributions for its finance. Some local authorities made grants, Rotary Clubs and some local businesses also contributed. For many years, Ivan Carr was a member of the committee and workers at his family's flour mill in Silloth all contributed a day's pay to the funds each

24

year. In 1990, the home received £3,300 from the BBC's Children in Need appeal. This was used to install an all-weather surface in the playground.

Major Antony Harrison, a grandson of the founder, came to live locally in 1971 and was invited to join the committee. He saw a steady demand for holidays at the home over the next twenty years.

Then, in 1990, there was an unpleasant incident. The mother of two boys from West Cumberland complained of ill-treatment of one of her sons by a member of staff. The police and Social Services became involved and the home was immediately closed. Although the police found no evidence to support the allegations, the committee instituted a full review of the home's activities.

It had become increasingly difficult to find suitable staff and, finally, Mrs Margaret Rickman, who had inherited the property from her grandmother, agreed to closure. The building was sold for around a quarter-of-a-million pounds. This sum was added to the existing trust fund and used to form the Harrison Charity.

This trust now provides grants to children and young people in need, hardship or distress to provide holidays and trips. Among other things, they finance Skiing holidays to France and Outward Bound activities in the Lake District. They carry on the original aims of the home's founders with a very definite 21st Century accent!

A fancy-dress event in the 1980's

25

A walk round the village

1. Start your walk in the car park by the bridge and turn towards the sea. The block of buildings on your left included two of Allonby's many pubs. The Grapes and The Solway Hotel which stood on the corner and was demolished following a fire in the 1990s. The lane between the houses originally led to the Beeby family's fish yards **(PAGE 10)**.

Walk up to the cycle path and turn left, heading towards the church. Enjoy the view.

2. Cross the main road to Christ Church **(PAGE 19)**. There are some interesting inscriptions on the headstones in the churchyard although many have suffered damage from the Solway weather. Leave the church and head back to the centre of the village.

3. The West Winds tearoom was originally the vicarage, built in 1872. In the 1950s, it became a holiday home for children suffering from cerebral palsy. It was a hotel and then a private home for some years before its present incarnation. Continue along the road.

4 . Twentymans is famous throughout North Cumbria for its ice cream – made on the premises from a secret family recipe. The pictures in the windows show how the business has developed since 1920 when it was founded. Take the path away from the road, past the houses and then turn up the cobbled lane just beyond the bus shelter – Brewery Street.

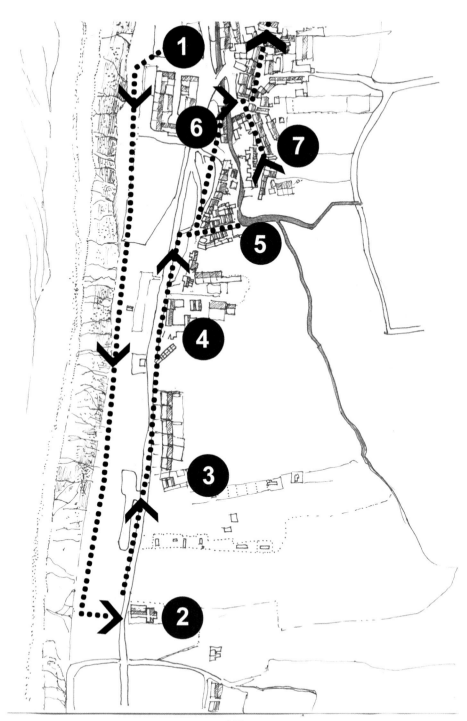

5. Walk to the end of the lane. This lane was part of the main street through the village before the present coast road was built. Today, the beck blocks the way forward but there was originally a ford here; in those days, the beck was much wider and more shallow. Little is known about the brewery which gave the street its name. You will pick up the rest of the street, later in the walk. Walk back to the path and follow it along past the houses.

6. The large, sandstone building, now an antiques shop, was Allonby Mill **(PAGE 6)**. The building has been much altered over the years. Just beyond the shop, take the modern foot bridge over the beck. The building facing you was The Queen's Head Inn and then, in the mid-1800s, became Allonby's first and only Temperance Hotel. Turn right into Garden Lane.

7. You are now back on the cobbled main street which ran from the ford at the end of Brewery Street. On your left is Rainford House **(PAGE 7)**. Walk back up Garden Lane, and take the narrow, cobbled alley at the back of 'Riverside'. It's just wide enough for a horse but you'd never get the cart through! Cross the road to Westnewton with care and carry on along the old cobbled street. Note the date stone on 'Bridge House'. This may have been moved from an earlier structure and probably refers to the Martindales, one of Allonby's early Quaker families.

Rainford House

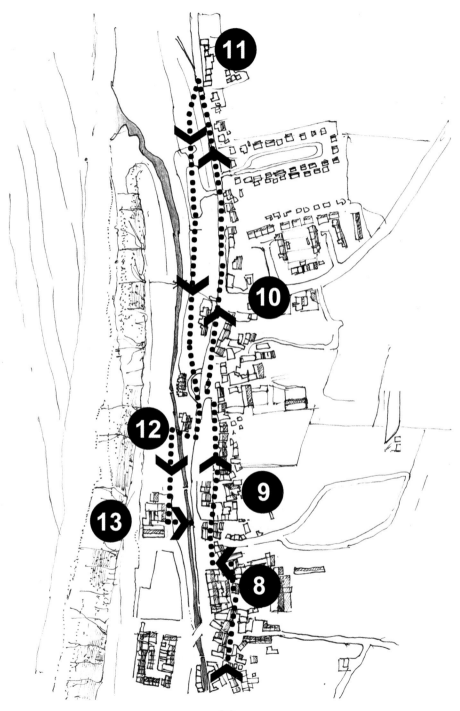

8. You are now in 'The Square' behind the Ship Hotel. There were two more pubs here – The Sun and the Swan; can you spot any clues as to where they were located? Follow the cobbles out onto the verge of the main road, past the tea room, operated by the Stordy family for many years. Pass behind the large building, formally the Central Garage, and enter the second part of the square.

9. You can now see the impressive portico of the baths. (**PAGE 12**) and opposite it 'Allonby Grange' which was home to Anne Satterthwaite who inherited most of the Beeby estate. **(PAGE 10)** When Anne's only son died, her daughter-in-law, Sarah, remarried in 1882. The groom was James Clark, founder of Clark's shoes, from Street in Somerset.

Continue along the cobbles and cross Moss Lane which leads to the modern Leisure Centre and the school.

10. The building straight ahead was the Congregational Chapel. Behind this is the old Sunshine Home (**PAGE 24**) and, beyond that the single-storey building which was the Quaker Meeting House (**PAGE 6**). Carry on along the road, passing Percy Foster's Field, one of the very first caravan sites in the area.

11 . You are now at North Lodge (**PAGE 18**). The modern house in front of it was the Police Station and, beyond the lodge, surrounded by a high wall, is the Friends' Burial Ground. Cross the road, walk diagonally across the car park and then follow the beck back toward the centre of the village, passing several recently gentrified houses, then head back towards the road.

12. You have now arrived at the beautifully restored Reading Rooms (**PAGE 16**). Walk around the front and then along the edge of the road to the footbridge. Cross back to the green and head for the cluster of buildings straight ahead.

13. These buildings are known as the Hill. Over the years, they have housed many different businesses. Yet another pub, The Spirit Vaults, was located here. The landlord was Alfred Costin whose family also ran the Kipper Smoke House (**PAGE 8**) which was located in the three storey white house at the far end of the block. In more recent times, Allonby Riding School and Stables was here. Head back towards the road and go over the footbridge.

The Ship Inn awaits you! Look at the blue plaque to see in whose footsteps you are treading.

The Zoologist Vicar

Rev. Hugh Alexander Macpherson was the vicar of Allonby between 1896 and 1900. He was a prominent naturalist and wrote several books. He published both *"Vertebrate Fauna of Lakeland"* and *"Red Deer: Natural History, Deer Stalking, Stag Hunting and Cookery"* in 1892.

He became the first honorary Director of Zoology at Tullie House when the museum opened in 1893. He donated many specimens to the natural history collection there. Some of these are still on view including a Tuna Fish, washed ashore near Burgh in 1889. This fish is over two metres long and was transported to a taxidermist in Penrith to be stuffed. It yielded 28 stone (183Kg) of flesh which was offered to anyone in the town who cared to try it.

After leaving Allonby, Rev. Macpherson took charge of the Episcopalian church at Pitlochry in Scotland. He died there, shortly afterwards, at the age of forty-three.

Rev. Macpherson, in the pony and trap, and some locals investigate the carcass of a Bottlenose Whale, washed ashore at Beckfoot in 1897.

I am deeply indebted to the other members of the Holme St. Cuthbert History Group for much of the information contained in this booklet. In particular the research carried out by Karen Simpson and Stephen Wright has been invaluable.

I must also thank Denis Perriam, Antony Harrison, Lord Inglewood, Dennis Irwin, Pam Jones, Felix Stirling and Bobby Watson who have been very generous with information, pictures and encouragement. There is more information on Allonby at: http://www.allonbycumbria.co.uk/